SUPREME COURT CASES

THROUGH PRIMARY SOURCES™

Roe V. Wade

The Right to Choose

Simone Payment

rosen central
Primary Source™
The Rosen Publishing Group, Inc., New York

Published in 2004 by The Rosen Publishing Group, Inc.
29 East 21st Street, New York, NY 10010

Library of Congress Cataloging-in-Publication Data

Payment, Simone.
Roe v. Wade : the right to choose / by Simone Payment. — 1st ed.
    p. cm. — (Supreme Court cases through primary sources)
Includes bibliographical references and index.
Contents: A historic case begins in Texas—Abortion goes on trial—Next stop, Supreme Court—Another trip to the Supreme Court—Finally, a decision—After Roe v. Wade.
ISBN 0-8239-4012-8 (library binding)
1. Roe, Jane, 1947– —Trials, litigation, etc.—Juvenile literature.
2. Wade, Henry—Trials, litigation, etc.—Juvenile literature. 3. Trials (Abortion)—Washington, (D.C.)—Juvenile literature. 4. Abortion— Law and legislation—United States—Juvenile literature. [1. Roe, Jane, 1947– —Trials, litigation, etc. 2. Wade, Henry—Trials, litigation, etc. 3. Trials (Abortion) 4. Abortion—Law and legislation] I. Title. II. Title: Roe versus Wade. III. Series.
KF228.R59P39 2004
342.73'084—dc21

                                                    2002155346

Manufactured in the United States of America

Contents

Introduction   4

1. **A Historic Case Begins in Texas**   7

2. **Abortion Goes on Trial**   16

3. **Next Stop: Supreme Court**   25

4. **Another Trip to the Supreme Court**   37

5. **Finally, a Decision**   42

6. **After *Roe v. Wade***   47

Glossary   53

For More Information   55

For Further Reading   56

Bibliography   57

Primary Source Image List   59

Index   60

Introduction

Abortion has always been a controversial issue. On one side of the debate are people who believe that abortion is murder. Other people believe that a woman should have a legal right to choose whether to have a child. In 1973, these two groups lined up on opposing sides of a Supreme Court case that became known as *Roe v.* [versus] *Wade*.

Roe v. Wade came about because women were being denied the right to choose what they did with their bodies. In states all across America, abortion was illegal in most cases. The laws forced some women into dangerous situations if they decided to get an abortion illegally. Sometimes, women died as a result of unsafe illegal abortions. Some women even tried to end their pregnancies themselves. Others chose to go to other countries to get a safe, legal abortion. Most women, however, could not afford to do that.

The question of when life begins is the basis for the conflict between supporters of the right to choose and people who are against abortion. The photo on the left depicts pro-choice marchers picketing outside a 1979 antiabortion convention in Fort Mitchell, Kentucky. On the other side of the issue, shown in the 1976 photo on the right, a man in Massachusetts holds a sign that states, "Abortion Is Murder."

A group of women in Texas were unhappy with this situation. They thought every woman should be able to choose what happened to her body. The group decided to try to change the laws to give women that right. In 1970, they found two young lawyers who were willing to try to legalize abortion. The lawyers decided to challenge the abortion law in Texas. They found a young woman who wanted to end her pregnancy and who was willing to stand for all other pregnant women in Texas who wanted an abortion. To protect her privacy, she was known as Jane Roe.

The case went all the way to the Supreme Court. Lawyers for the state of Texas believed that the current laws should remain. They believed that the mother should give up her rights because the rights of the fetus are more important. Jane Roe's lawyers argued that all women had a right to privacy, including choosing to end a pregnancy. The case was one of the most controversial in U.S. history and is still debated today.

A Historic Case Begins in Texas

1

In her autobiography, *A Question of Choice*, Sarah Weddington wrote, "*Roe v. Wade* started at a garage sale." It might seem like a strange place for such an important case to begin. Although *Roe v. Wade* may have started small, it soon caught the attention of the entire country.

A SHORT HISTORY OF ABORTION

Abortion is the termination of a pregnancy. Abortion was practiced as long ago as the time of the ancient societies of Greece, Rome, and Egypt. Women used common plants to stop their pregnancies if, for example, their family could not afford to care for another child.

Women in the early days of the United States also used abortion to end pregnancies. By the mid-1800s, it was

Margaret Sanger, the founder of the American Birth Control League, urged courts to grant doctors the right to give advice about methods of birth control in hospitals and clinics. The American Birth Control League later became Planned Parenthood, which is still active today.

fairly common. As many as one out of five pregnancies was ended by an abortion. At that time, abortion was not a crime. Beginning in Connecticut in 1821, however, states began to pass laws about abortion. Doctors wanted to make certain that the procedure was safe for women. They also wanted to try to prevent women from giving themselves abortions. Other doctors objected for moral reasons. They believed that it was wrong to kill unborn children.

Attitudes about abortion began to change late in the 1800s, and forty states banned the procedure. It did not become less common though. Women found doctors who would give them illegal abortions, or they would try to do it themselves. Both options were very dangerous, and many women died or were seriously hurt from procedures that did not work. This concerned doctors and women's groups, and by the mid-1900s, they began to work hard to change the laws. Also, as medical science advanced and there were better tests, women sometimes knew ahead of time if their babies would be born with a birth defect or other problems because of a disease. Doctors wanted to give women the option of ending these pregnancies.

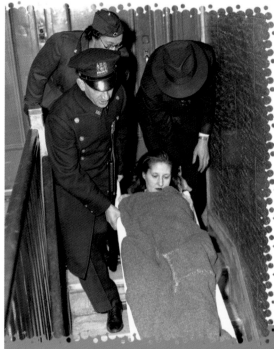

Authorities carry a woman out of her doctor's apartment after she tried to get an illegal abortion in 1944. Dr. Louis Solomon was in the middle of the operation in his kitchen when the police raided his apartment. Illegal, or "back alley," abortions were often the cause of dangerous infections and life-threatening bleeding in women.

Some states began to change laws in cases where a mother's life was in danger if the pregnancy continued, or if the pregnancy was the result of rape. By 1967, a few states had laws that allowed abortion. However, there were strict rules about when an abortion could be performed. Usually, a woman needed the approval of one or more doctors to get an abortion. Because of these restrictions, many women had illegal abortions and problems remained. Groups like Planned Parenthood began to fight for laws that were less strict.

THE

PENAL CODE

OF

THE STATE OF TEXAS.

ADOPTED BY THE SIXTH LEGISLATURE

GALVESTON:
PRINTED AT THE NEWS OFFICE.
1857.

CHAPTER VII.

OF ABORTION.

ARTICLE 531. If any person shall designedly administer to a pregnant woman, with her consent, any drug or medicine, or shall use towards her any violence, or any means whatever, externally or internally applied, and shall thereby procure an abortion, he shall be punished, by confinement, in the Penitentiary, not less than two, nor more than five years; if it be done without her consent the punishment shall be doubled.

ART. 532. Any person who furnishes the means for procuring an abortion, knowing the purpose intended, is guilty as an accomplice.

ART. 533. If the means used shall fail to produce an abortion, the offender is nevertheless guilty of an attempt to procure abortion, provided it be shown that such means were calculated to produce that result, and shall receive one-half the punishment prescribed in Article 531.

This is a copy of the cover of The Penal Code of the State of Texas, *found at the Texas State Library in Austin, Texas. According to Chapter VII, Article 531 (right), "If any person shall designedly administer to a pregnant woman, with her consent, any drug or medicine, or shall use towards her any violence, or any means whatever . . . and shall thereby procure an abortion, he shall be punished . . ."*

THE LAW IN TEXAS

The first abortion law in Texas was passed in 1857. The laws were changed over the years and became much more strict. By 1970, the only way a woman could have an abortion in Texas was if her life was at risk from the pregnancy. As a result of these strict laws, many women in Texas went to Mexico to get abortions. It was legal there, but it was not always safe, and it was not cheap. Poor women usually could not afford to travel there for the procedure.

A group in Austin, Texas, called the Women's Liberation Birth Control Information Center, wanted to help women find safe abortions. They had a telephone hot line women could call for information on how to find a doctor to perform a safe abortion. The group worried that they could get into legal trouble for helping these women. They turned to Sarah Weddington for help.

A YOUNG LAWYER TO THE RESCUE

Sarah Weddington was a smart young lawyer who had recently graduated from the University of Texas Law School. She had finished both college and law school a year early, so she was only twenty-four years old. She

At the age of twenty-six, Sarah Weddington was the youngest woman ever to win a case before the United States Supreme Court. Weddington would go on to become a Texas state legislator and, at the time of this photo, a top aide for women's issues at the White House.

was very active in women's groups. One Saturday morning in 1969 at a garage sale, some of her friends asked for her help. They worked for the group in Austin trying to help women get safe abortions. They wanted her to do some legal research to find out whether they could be prosecuted for their actions.

Weddington agreed to help and began spending her spare time researching legal cases. She looked at cases from all over the United States and found some she thought could help them. Weddington believed that the time was right to challenge Texas's law on abortion.

When Weddington reported her findings to her friends, they were very encouraged. They were impressed with what she had done and asked her to put together a legal case to challenge the law. At first, Weddington was uncertain. In her autobiography, she recalls telling the group, "No, you need someone older and with more experience." She had never even argued a case in court. The group assured her that she was the right person for the job. She thought more about it and decided she was ready for the challenge.

A PERSONAL EXPERIENCE

Something else helped Sarah Weddington make up her mind to take the case. When she was in law school, she became pregnant. She was not yet married to Ron Weddington, the man who later became her husband. Both of them were students and did not have enough money to raise a child. Weddington made the painful choice to have an abortion. She and Ron used all the money they had to travel to Mexico to have it done. Although Weddington was lucky and got a clean and safe abortion, she remembered how scared and ashamed she had been. She did not want other women to go through that same experience.

COFFEE JOINS THE TEAM

Weddington knew she had a lot of work to do. She already had a full-time job and was working on the case for free. Knowing she could not do it alone, she called Linda Coffee. Coffee had been in Weddington's class in law school. Coffee and Weddington had been two of only five women in their class. Like Weddington, Coffee was very smart. She had gotten top honors in law school and earned one of the highest grades on the bar,

Shown here preparing for a case in 1972, attorney Linda Coffee was a crucial member of the Roe v. Wade *team. Coffee was the first to speak at the initial trial in Dallas. She was also instrumental in persuading the Texas Supreme Court to dismiss the state's filing fee for elections.*

the exam lawyers must pass to practice law. After law school, Coffee worked as a law clerk for a judge, then at a small law firm in Dallas, Texas.

Coffee was interested in what Weddington had to say. She was interested in issues that affected women and agreed to work with Weddington on the abortion case. Like Weddington, she would not receive any money for her work and would need to spend a lot of her free time on the case.

FINDING ROE

The first thing Weddington and Coffee had to do was find a plaintiff, someone who had been affected by the existing law and would represent their cause. In this case, it needed to be a woman who wanted an abortion but who was not able to get one. Weddington and Coffee found their plaintiff when a young, pregnant woman named Norma McCorvey approached a lawyer for help. She was unmarried and very poor, and she knew she would not be able to care for a baby. She had tried to get an abortion but could not find a doctor to perform one. McCorvey finally did find someone who performed abortions, but he was not a doctor and charged $500. McCorvey was afraid to go to this man. She had heard many stories about bad things that had happened to women who had gotten illegal abortions.

McCorvey's lawyer knew about the lawsuit Coffee and Weddington were trying to file. He thought McCorvey would be a good plaintiff for their case. The two women arranged to meet McCorvey at a pizza parlor in Dallas. They listened to her story and explained to her what they were looking for. They assured her that she would not have to go to court herself. They would not use her real name, and she did not have to pay them.

There was one major problem though: The court system moves slowly. By the time the case was decided, it would probably be too late for McCorvey to get an abortion. McCorvey agreed to become the plaintiff anyway. She hoped the case would help other women even if it did not help her.

Weddington and Coffee had McCorvey sign a legal document called an affidavit. It stated that McCorvey was pregnant and wanted an abortion but could not get one. Because she did not want her real name used, in the document McCorvey was referred to as Jane Roe.

Abortion Goes on Trial

2

Now that Weddington and Coffee had a plaintiff, they began working on their case. Both had other jobs, but they worked hard doing research at night and on weekends. They wanted to finish their research as quickly as possible so that McCorvey would still be pregnant when they filed their case.

McCorvey had not broken a law. In Texas, it was not illegal for a woman to try to get an abortion or even to give herself one. It was illegal to perform an abortion on someone else. Weddington and Coffee knew they needed to base their case on the fact that the law did not allow McCorvey access to a safe abortion from a medical doctor.

They also wanted to base their case on the fact that there was a law that was more important than Texas law: the Constitution of the United States. Weddington and Coffee believed that the state of Texas was violating the

Constitution because its abortion law interfered with a woman's right to privacy. They believed this right was guaranteed in the U.S. Constitution.

THE CONSTITUTION AND THE RIGHT TO PRIVACY

Most of the U.S. legal system is based on the Constitution and its amendments. Some of our rights and freedoms are spelled out in the Constitution and its amendments, such as the freedom of speech

Years after her landmark Supreme Court case, Norma McCorvey takes a break from her job as a house painter to pose for this January 1983 photograph. To keep her identity a secret, McCorvey's lawyers referred to her as "Jane Roe" when McCorvey decided to become the plaintiff in the case.

and the right to vote. Other rights are not spelled out but are suggested, such as the right to privacy. Many lawyers and people who study the Constitution and amendments believe that right was part of the original intention of the Constitution.

Justice Louis Brandeis, a member of the Supreme Court in 1928, called this the "right to be let alone." He wrote that it was what the founding fathers of the United States were looking for when they left England. They believed that this right was so obvious it did not need to be included in the Constitution. Later, the Ninth Amendment was added to the Constitution. Its purpose

In this image of a 1972 pro-choice demonstration in New York City, women march arm-in-arm and express their desire to have a right to choose. The banner in the center states, "A Woman's Right to Choose Abortion. Defend the Right to Abortion in N.Y." Behind them, to the left, another banner proclaims in French, "Laissez Faire," which means, in this case, "let us do it."

was to add liberties not already spelled out in the Constitution. Justice Brandeis and others have argued that the right to privacy is covered in this amendment and several others.

MAKING THEIR CASE

In their research, Weddington and Coffee found other legal cases that helped them put together their own case. The most important of these cases, one called *Griswold v. Connecticut*, had been decided by the Supreme Court in 1965. It said that married couples had the right to use contraceptives to prevent pregnancy.

They had the right to privacy and should be able to make their own decisions. The *Griswold* decision was based on the First, Third, Fourth, Fifth, Ninth, and Fourteenth Amendments to the United States Constitution.

Weddington and Coffee knew that the right to privacy was key to their case. The legal documents they wrote said that the current Texas law interfered with a woman's right to get advice about abortion from her doctor. The law also interfered with her right to choose whether to have a child. Their legal document—called a brief—used the First, Fourth, Fifth, Ninth, and Fourteenth Amendments to make their case.

Coffee filed their case on March 3, 1970, at the courthouse in Dallas. Weddington and Coffee had decided that their case should go to a federal court, rather than a Texas court. This was because there were constitutional issues at stake. If the federal court agreed that the Texas law was unconstitutional, laws in other states could change as well.

After the case was filed, Weddington and Coffee realized that they needed to make the case a class action lawsuit. This meant that it would apply to many people, not only Roe. They added the words "and all others similarly situated" to the lawsuit. This would be important if Roe was no longer pregnant when the case finally went to court. Then the case could still apply to any woman who was pregnant and wanted an abortion.

WADE ENTERS THE PICTURE

Now that the case was officially filed with the court, Roe had an opponent. Henry Wade was the Dallas County district attorney,

IMPORTANT AMENDMENTS

Weddington and Coffee used several amendments to help make their case:

- The **First** specifies the right "to petition the government for a redress of grievances." This gave Jane Roe the right to file her case.

- The **Fourth** gives U.S. citizens the right "to be secure . . . against unreasonable searches and seizures." This means that the government does not have the right to be involved in a citizen's business without good reason. This is one of the main amendments used to prove the right to privacy.

- The **Fifth** allows protection from being "deprived of life, liberty, or property, without due process of law." This also gave Roe the right to file her case.

- The **Ninth** states that there are rights not specifically listed in the Constitution that citizens are entitled to. This is another amendment used to show that the right to privacy is included in the Constitution.

- The **Fourteenth** says, "No State shall make or enforce any laws which shall abridge the privileges . . . of citizens of the United States; . . . nor deny . . . the equal protection of laws." In other words, states shouldn't be able to pass any laws that keep a woman from having the right to privacy.

To read more about all twenty-seven amendments to the Constitution, please go to http://www.infoplease.com/ipa/A0749825.html.

the person in charge of prosecuting all cases in Dallas. He and his office would represent the state of Texas in the case.

Wade did not think there was much to the case. There had been other cases that challenged Texas's abortion law, but none had been successful. He did not think *Roe v. Wade* would be any different.

Wade put John Tolle in charge of the case. Like Wade, Tolle did not believe that the *Roe* case would change the Texas law. Tolle did not think the case should even go to trial. The Texas

District attorney of Dallas County, Texas, Henry Wade poses in his office in the early 1970s. Wade's career spanned thirty-five years. In addition to Roe v. Wade, Wade also prosecuted Jack Ruby, the man responsible for shooting Lee Harvey Oswald, President John. F. Kennedy's alleged assassin.

law did not punish pregnant women, only doctors that performed abortions. Therefore, Tolle believed Roe should not even be filing a case.

When thinking about the case, Tolle overlooked the fact that society was changing quickly in the late 1960s and early 1970s. The women's movement was gaining momentum, and people were thinking about whether the rights of the mother or the fetus were more important. Weddington and Coffee's case was based on the opinion that the rights of the mother are more important.

Tolle saw things differently. He began doing medical research about abortion and came to believe that the fetus had a right to life. To him, that right was more important than the rights of the mother. He based his case on that idea and believed that would be enough to win. He did not mention anything about the woman's right to privacy in his response to the *Roe v. Wade* case, which was filed on March 23, 1970.

ROE V. WADE IS ARGUED IN TEXAS

Two months later, the case went to court. On May 22, reporters crowded into the courtroom, along with friends and supporters of both sides. The case was heard by a three-judge panel of the federal district court, specially appointed by John R. Brown, the chief judge of the Fifth Circuit Federal Court.

Coffee began by discussing why she was asking the court to change the Texas law. She was also asking for Texas to stop enforcing the current law. Weddington argued next. Texas was trying to protect the fetus and its rights, but Weddington explained that this was not legally possible. No laws gave a fetus legal rights, and this case was no different. Weddington said the state should be more concerned with protecting the rights of women. If doctors performed safe abortions, there was no reason for the state to try to stop them.

WHAT ABOUT NORMA McCORVEY?

The decision in the *Roe v. Wade* case came too late for Norma McCorvey. Soon after the decision in the Texas case, she gave birth to a baby girl. McCorvey put the baby up for adoption immediately after the birth. It is interesting to note that McCorvey never actually had an abortion, even though the name she was known as—Jane Roe— now represents the right to abortion.

Next, it was Tolle's turn to speak. He admitted that no one was quite certain when life began, but he said that the state should have the "right to protect life . . . in whatever stage it may be in." He argued that the state must think about the rights of the mother and fetus. Then the state should find the proper balance of those rights. He told the judges, "[T]he state's position . . . is that the right of the child to life is superior to [a] woman's right to privacy."

THE COURT'S DECISION

A few weeks later, the court made a decision. It read, "[T]he plaintiffs argue . . . that the Texas abortion laws must be declared unconstitutional because they deprive . . . women . . . of their right, secured by the Ninth Amendment, to choose whether or not to have children. We agree." This was a victory for Roe, but the victory was not complete. Nothing in the ruling said that Texas had to stop enforcing the law. Wade told reporters his office planned to continue prosecuting doctors. Women were still not able to get abortions in Texas because doctors could not perform them.

Next Stop: Supreme Court

3

Weddington and Coffee were pleased with the federal court's ruling. However, they knew this was not the end of the case. They needed to appeal the case to a higher court. An appeal is a request for another court to take a case. Usually a lawyer needs to appeal to higher and higher courts to eventually get to the Supreme Court. In the case of *Roe v. Wade*, Weddington and Coffee were able to go directly to the Supreme Court. This was because, even though the federal court had said the Texas law was unconstitutional, Texas planned to ignore the ruling. Because Texas was planning to go against the court's decision, the Supreme Court could step in and make a ruling.

As the highest court in the United States, the Supreme Court has the power to decide whether a law or action of the government goes against the Constitution.

Many of the important issues in the history of the United States have been decided by the Supreme Court. Any decision the Court makes can be changed only by a later Supreme Court ruling or by a new amendment to the Constitution.

Weddington and Coffee filed a petition for certiorari, a document asking the Supreme Court to hear the case. *Roe v. Wade* was one of thousands of petitions filed that year. Most of those cases never made it to the Supreme Court. The nine justices who make up the Supreme Court vote on whether to take a case. If there is a majority, the case is accepted. In this case, five of the nine justices of the Supreme Court agreed to hear *Roe v. Wade*.

On May 3, 1971, the Supreme Court announced that it had agreed to take *Roe v. Wade*. It became one of approximately 150 cases heard by the Court that year.

EACH SIDE PREPARES FOR THE SUPREME COURT

Coffee and Weddington immediately began preparing their case for the Supreme Court. When a case is argued at the Supreme Court, lawyers have only thirty minutes to speak. In other kinds of cases, lawyers can argue as long as they want and can call witnesses to support their case. Because Coffee and Weddington would have only a short time at the Supreme Court, it was important that their brief be well prepared. The justices would read the brief before the trial.

Most of the information they learned about the case came from the brief.

Preparing the brief took a great deal of time. Coffee had a full-time job and was unable to help much. Weddington had to quit her job at the city attorney's office in Fort Worth, Texas. Her boss did not want her spending her time working on "women's lib" issues. At first, she did not know what to do. She was still working on the *Roe* case for free. Preparing the brief, making copies, and filing the case would be expensive. Fortunately, a lawyer named Roy Lucas offered a solution. He worked at the James Madison Constitutional Law Institute in New York City. He was interested in trying to strike down abortion laws in New York. When abortion was legalized in New York State in 1970, he began looking at cases in other parts of the country. Lucas heard about *Roe v. Wade* and offered to help Weddington and Coffee. He knew *Roe* was an important case.

With the help of Lucas and the lawyers at the institute, Weddington flew to New York City to continue her research. There was so much to be done that Weddington's husband, Ron, also a lawyer, joined her in New York to help her with the case.

Finally, after many long months of research, the brief was completed and submitted to the Court on August 17, 1971. It had grown to 139 pages and had a 500-page appendix. The appendix was filled with tables, charts, and graphs with information on abortion.

In addition to the brief, forty-two other briefs were submitted. These briefs are called amicus curiae briefs, which means "friends of the court." Written by groups like the American Civil Liberties Union and Planned Parenthood, they helped to support the information in Weddington and Coffee's brief.

With the brief finished, Weddington began practicing for her day in court. She went to see another case argued at the Supreme Court to see what it was like. Weddington also practiced in moot courts, similar to doing a dress rehearsal for a play. Weddington argued her case in front of professors, law students, and friends playing the part of justices. They asked the types of questions they thought the Supreme Court justices might ask.

In Dallas, Henry Wade assigned Jay Floyd to work on the Texas brief. Their position would be similar to the one in the original case. They considered the fetus to be a human being from the moment of conception (when the sperm fertilizes the egg). They believed the fetus's right to life was more important than the rights of the mother to make the decision.

Floyd was very busy working on other cases their office was handling. He did not have much time to devote to the case. He was able to get help from two lawyers in Chicago. Jerome Frazel and Dennis Horan put together a brief that used medical evidence from doctors. Floyd was able to use many parts of their work in his brief, but he added his own introduction.

There were several amicus curiae briefs filed to support Texas's case. A medical group submitted a brief stating that a fetus should be considered a patient, the same as the mother. A lawyer's group submitted a brief discussing existing laws on abortion.

Finally, Texas's brief and the amicus curiae briefs were submitted to the Supreme Court on October 15, 1971. Now everyone involved had to wait for his or her day in court.

THE BIG DAY

Roe v. Wade was scheduled to be heard by the Supreme Court on December 13, 1971. The upcoming hearing brought lots of attention to the abortion issue. Groups on both sides of the debate organized protests and marches. Both groups had protesters outside the Supreme Court on the morning of the hearing.

Weddington arrived early on the day of the hearing. Coffee was there as well, but only Weddington would be speaking. Each side could have only one lawyer present the case. Most of the thirty minutes each side had would be taken up by the Supreme Court justices asking the lawyers questions. The justices ask questions to get more information on points made in the brief. They also sometimes use their questions to try to convince other justices of a point. In some cases, they even use their questions to show lawyers weak points in their cases.

If you can't trust me with a choice, how can you trust me with a child?

Roe v. Wade

The interior of the United States Supreme Court is rarely seen by the public. The 1970s saw a wave of women's issues reach the Court, including Reed v. Reed in 1971. In that case, the Court ruled that the choice of administrator for an estate "may not lawfully be mandated solely on the basis of sex." In 1973, the Court invalidated a law that provided better housing and medical benefits for males in the military than for females. In 1974, the Court upheld an equal-pay-for-equal-work statute.

Seven justices waited in the courtroom to hear *Roe v. Wade*: Harry Blackmun, William Brennan, Warren Burger, William Douglas, Thurgood Marshall, Potter Stewart, and Byron White. Usually there are nine justices, but two had recently resigned because of health problems. Justices are appointed by the current president and must be approved by Congress. This can be a long process, so open positions are not always filled immediately.

The courtroom where *Roe* was heard was decorated with marble, red velvet curtains, and dark wood paneling. The justices wore black robes and sat at a long bench in front of the lawyers.

This photo, from the personal collection of Sarah Weddington, was taken on December 13, 1971, the day that the U.S. Supreme Court heard the first arguments of Roe v. Wade. *Standing left to right are Ron Weddington, Sarah Weddington, U.S. Representative George Mahon, and Lena Katharine Ragle, Sarah's mother.*

The room was filled with reporters, guests of each lawyer, and regular people who had waited in line for a chance to hear this important case.

Weddington was the first to speak. She began by going over a brief history of the case. The justices interrupted her from time to time to ask questions. She talked to the justices about pregnancy from a woman's perspective. "It disrupts her body, it disrupts her education, it disrupts her employment . . . [T]his certainly . . . is a matter . . . of such fundamental and basic concern for the woman involved that she should be allowed to make the choice as to whether to continue or terminate her pregnancy."

Next, Weddington reminded the justices that the federal court had decided that a woman's right to an abortion was based on the Ninth Amendment. She added that she believed that right was also based on the Fourteenth Amendment "under the rights of persons to life [and] liberty. . . . [In this case] liberty from being forced to continue the unwanted pregnancy."

Another important point Weddington wanted to make was that the fetus did not have legal rights under the Constitution. The Constitution only begins protecting the rights of citizens when they are born.

After twenty-five minutes, Weddington's time was up. She wanted to save her last five minutes to respond to any points Floyd might make in his argument.

LADIES' DAY

December 13, 1971, was called "Ladies' Day" by the staff of the Supreme Court. In addition to Weddington's arguing for *Roe*, Margie Pitts Hames and Dorothy Beasley argued on opposing sides of another case heard that day, *Doe v. Bolton*. This was an unusual occurrence at the time. Not many women were lawyers, and very few had argued a case in the Supreme Court. In fact, there was not even a women's rest room in the lounge where lawyers waited before entering the courtroom.

Next Stop: Supreme Court

Floyd began his presentation with a joke: "[W]hen a man argues against two beautiful ladies like this, they're going to have the last word." Unfortunately for Floyd, no one found his joke funny.

Floyd's first point was that Jane Roe should not be bringing the case to court because she was no longer pregnant. One of the justices reminded Floyd that the case was a class action, representing all the pregnant women in Texas. There are "at any given time unmarried pregnant females in the State of Texas," said the justice. Floyd was uncertain about how to respond. Finally, he replied that a woman would not be able to have her case heard by the Supreme Court. By the time the case made it to the Supreme Court, her baby would already have been born. Floyd said there were some cases where courts simply could not fix the situation. However, this was exactly why the case was at the Supreme Court. The original ruling in the case gave the right to an abortion, but there was no way to get a decision made in a Texas state court. Maybe a woman made her choice about whether to have an abortion, "when she decides to live in Texas," said one of the justices, only half joking. This made Floyd a little angry and he replied, "There is no restriction on moving [to another state]." Whether Floyd knew it or not, he had made a good point for the other side. Many women did not have enough money to go to another state—or another country—to get a legal abortion.

One of the justices then asked Floyd why Texas wanted to ban abortions except in a few cases. Floyd said it was to protect the life of the fetus. This made a justice ask why Texas never prosecuted mothers who got abortions, only people who gave abortions. He reminded Floyd that Texas had originally passed

This photo of a billboard along Route 66 in McGrann, Pennsylvania, taken on April 13, 1971, reads: "Legal Abortions. (212) 490-3600. Usually under $250." The bottom of the sign lists the company's postal address in New York City. New York State legalized abortion in 1970, and it was a nearby place for Pennsylvania residents who were seeking abortions to travel.

the law to protect mothers from abortionists. Why was Floyd now saying that Texas was trying to protect the fetus? Floyd had to agree that the justice asked a good question.

The justices had a few more questions: When should the state step in to protect the fetus, rather than the mother? When did the state believe the life of the fetus begins? When did the rights of the fetus become more important than the mother's rights? Floyd answered that the rights of the fetus were always more important than the mother's rights. He said that the state believed the fetus began having rights "seven to nine days after conception." "What about six days?" asked a justice. Floyd was only able to answer, "We don't know . . . there are unanswerable questions in the field." As laughter broke out in the courtroom, Floyd knew things had not gone well. His thirty minutes were up.

THE JUSTICES DISCUSS THE CASE

The seven Supreme Court justices met to discuss the case three days after the trial. They met behind closed doors. Each justice had the chance to speak about the case. After they were done

Chief justice of the Supreme Court Warren Burger poses in front of the American flag in this photograph, taken in 1971. Burger served seventeen years as chief justice, the longest tenure in the twentieth century. He wrote more than 250 opinions, including landmark decisions that enhanced women's rights and strengthened the constitutional separation of powers.

discussing the case, they took a vote. Chief Justice Burger counted the votes and found that five of the justices (including himself) were in favor of *Roe*. This was a majority, so it looked as though Roe had won. It turned out that it was not that simple.

The next thing the justices had to do was write what is called an opinion. This is an official explanation of their decision and why they made it. One justice is assigned to write the opinion. If other justices agree with it but have different reasons for their decision, they can write what is called a concurring opinion. Justices who disagree with the decision can write a dissent. When all opinions have been written, the majority opinion is released to the public.

Justice Blackmun was assigned to write the majority opinion. He was nervous about writing this important decision. It was the first major opinion he had been assigned. He knew abortion was a controversial issue. He began working on his opinion, carefully studying medical information and other legal decisions. Finally, five months after they had heard the case, Blackmun sent his draft to the other justices. The other justices did not feel it was strong enough. Blackmun spent another week working on it. The justices felt this one was better; however, Chief Justice Burger did not think it was good enough. They were not finished with this case.

Another Trip to the Supreme Court

4

In June 1972, Chief Justice Burger decided the Supreme Court needed to hear *Roe v. Wade* again. Two new justices, Lewis Powell and William Rehnquist, had joined the Court. They had not been part of the Court the first time the case was argued, and both were interested in hearing it. All but one of the other justices agreed, so the case was set to be heard again on October 11, 1972.

Weddington began her preparations for the Court that summer. She now had more support for her position because there were new abortion decisions in several other states. She could base parts of her brief on them. Floyd did not submit any new briefs.

A SECOND DAY IN COURT

At the second hearing, Weddington was the first to speak. She was even better prepared this time. She stated her case

Roe v. Wade

This Robert Oakes photograph shows the nine justices of the 1972 United States Supreme Court that voted on Roe v. Wade. *Back row, left to right: Justice Lewis Powell, Justice Thurgood Marshall, Justice Harry Blackmun, Justice William Rehnquist. Front row, left to right: Justice Potter Stewart, Justice William O. Douglas, Chief Justice Warren Burger, Justice William Brennan, and Justice Byron White.*

again, focusing on the importance of a woman's right to privacy. Weddington talked about how Texas women still needed to go to other states to get safe abortions. Doctors were still being punished for performing abortions.

Weddington quoted from other court decisions where states had agreed that the rights of the mother were more important than protecting the fetus. New York courts had decided that the fetus did not have rights according to the Constitution. One of the justices asked Weddington what would happen if the courts *did* decide the fetus had rights? Whose rights were more important? Weddington suggested that it might depend on the time of pregnancy. New York State had decided that after twenty-four weeks, the fetus's rights became more important. Weddington also admitted that if the courts decided the fetus had rights, she "would have a very difficult case."

When it was time for Texas's argument, Robert Flowers stepped up to present the case. He was Floyd's boss and was replacing Floyd for their second turn in the Court. Things had not gone well for their case the first time, and the team did not have high hopes that this appearance would be better.

Flowers began by stating his two main arguments. First, he believed the state should have a say in the life of the fetus, starting at conception. Second, deciding whose rights are more important should be up to state lawmakers.

One of the justices asked Flowers who should decide the question of when a fetus is considered a human being with rights. "Is it a legal question, a constitutional question, a medical question, a philosophical question, or a religious question, or what is it?" Flowers said the Supreme Court should decide based on the Constitution. A justice asked if Flowers thought the fetus should be considered a person. Flowers could not prove medically or legally that a fetus was a human starting at conception. He had to agree that if the fetus were not a person, Texas did not have a case.

WHY ROE V. WADE IS CALLED A "LANDMARK" DECISION...

In this cartoon by Steve Breen, drawn for the Asbury Park [New Jersey] Press, *an endless graveyard is shown with the words, "Why* Roe v. Wade *Is Called a 'Landmark' decision." Presumably, the artist is suggesting that* Roe v. Wade *will be the cause of many deaths—of unborn babies. He is making a play on words, using "landmark," which refers to important Supreme Court cases, to also mean a marker for graves.*

Flowers then told the Court that fetuses were a minority the state was trying to protect. "Who is speaking for these children? Where is the counsel [lawyer] for these unborn children, whose life is being taken?" When he was finished, Flowers did not think his case had gone well.

Weddington got the last word. She had saved five of her thirty minutes to respond to the state of Texas's case. She told the justices she knew how important this case was. It was a "case that must be decided on the Constitution." Weddington assured the Court that she was not trying to say that people should be in favor of abortion. "We do not ask this Court to rule

In contrast to the previous political cartoon, this drawing, "Cross Hairs," by Kevin Siers, makes a statement for the right-to-choose side of the abortion debate. This image was printed in the Charlotte Observer, *a North Carolina newspaper, in 1998. The bottom right-hand corner states, "Anti-Choice Terrorism." The picture is of a gun targeting "We the People . . ." This is the famous beginning of the United States Constitution. The cartoon suggests that enemies of the choice movement are attacking the basic rights of American citizens, as stated by the founding fathers in the Constitution.*

that abortion is good. We are here to [say] that the decision as to whether or not a particular woman will continue to carry or will terminate a pregnancy is a decision that should be made by the individual." Her closing speech stated that women should be free to make personal, private choices and not be told what to do by the government.

Finally, a Decision

In the months between hearings for the two cases, pollsters were asking people across the country what they thought. In a January 1972 Gallup poll, 57 percent of Americans said women and their doctors should make the decision to have an abortion. By August of that year, the number had risen to 64 percent. Vermont and New Jersey joined New York in legalizing abortion. Not everyone was in favor. In April 1972, the Catholic Knights of Columbus fraternal organization held a right-to-life rally. Ten thousand people attended to protest New York's new law on abortion.

THE CASE IS DECIDED

After hearing the case for the second time, the justices did not have any new information. Justice Blackmun still had not finished the opinion he started before the second hearing. The other justices were pushing for him to finish, but it was not until November 22—five weeks later—that he had a new draft.

Taken on February 4, 1974, in St. Paul, Minnesota, this photograph shows United States Supreme Court justice Harry Blackmun soon after he wrote the Roe v. Wade *majority opinion. Of the decision, Blackmun said, "[It] will be regarded as one of the worst mistakes in the Court's history or one of the greatest decisions . . ."*

The new draft suggested dividing a pregnancy into three parts, or trimesters. In the first three months, any woman could legally get an abortion. In the second and third trimesters, states could allow abortions with restrictions. The restrictions would be decided by each state. Several of the justices liked this new opinion. They suggested some changes to Blackmun, and he wrote a new draft. Now six of the other justices agreed with Blackmun's decision. Three of them wrote concurring opinions to show that they agreed with the decision but thought about it a little differently.

The remaining two justices dissented. They did not agree with Blackmun's opinion. Justice White disagreed strongly and said there was nothing in the Constitution that had anything to do with the right to an abortion. He thought making abortion legal was allowing mothers to make a decision based on whether or not it was convenient for them to have a child.

THE DECISION IS ANNOUNCED

On January 22, 1973, the decision was announced to the public. Justice Blackmun began his statement by saying he knew how important this issue was. Many people had very strong feelings on abortion. He said, "Our task, of course, is to resolve the issue by constitutional measurement, free of emotion."

The opinion explained the trimester system that allowed abortion for any woman in the first three months. In the second trimester, women could get a legal abortion. However, states could make rules that might limit abortion. After the second trimester, certain restrictions could be made. States would also have the option of making abortion illegal in the final trimester.

Blackmun's opinion went on to discuss the right to privacy. He agreed that it was not spelled out in the Constitution, but he said, "The Court has recognized that a right of personal privacy, or a guarantee of certain areas or zones of privacy, does exist under the Constitution." The mother's right to privacy becomes less important than the fetus's right to life only when the fetus could possibly survive outside the mother (at around six months).

The opinion also agreed with Weddington's point that rights given by the Fourteenth Amendment do not apply to a fetus. Laws do not apply to children not yet born. Justice Stewart wrote one of the concurring opinions. His opinion stated that the Fourteenth Amendment also protects the right to an abortion. It gives women the freedom to choose to end a pregnancy.

(Slip Opinion)

NOTE: Where it is deemed desirable, a syllabus (headnote) will be released, as is being done in connection with this case, at the time the opinion is issued. The syllabus constitutes no part of the opinion of the Court but has been prepared by the Reporter of Decisions for the convenience of the reader. See *United States v. Detroit Lumber Co.,* 200 U.S. 321, 337.

SUPREME COURT OF THE UNITED STATES

Syllabus

ROE ET AL. *v.* WADE, DISTRICT ATTORNEY OF
DALLAS COUNTY

APPEAL FROM THE UNITED STATES DISTRICT COURT FOR THE
NORTHERN DISTRICT OF TEXAS

No. 70–18.   Argued December 13, 1971—Reargued October 11,
1972—Decided January 22, 1973

From the collection of Sarah Weddington, here is a copy of the first page of the United States Supreme Court's final opinion regarding Roe v. Wade, *signed by the nine justices. Under the name of the case, this page states it is an "appeal from the United States district court for the northern district of Texas," and the dates the case was argued are also listed.*

Justice Rehnquist did not agree with the majority opinion. Like Justice White, he did not think abortion was protected by the Constitution. He believed it was not correct to base the decision on the right to privacy. After all, if you wanted an abortion, you needed to tell a doctor. You also needed to go to a hospital or a clinic. Therefore, it was not "private" at all. His dissent also stated that the Fourteenth Amendment should only protect people from losing freedom when laws were not followed.

The Supreme Court's decision surprised even supporters of the right to abortion. "Almost no one . . . expected the court

Telegram

western union

NO. WDS.—CL. OF SVC.	PD. OR COLL.	CASH NO.	CHARGE TO THE ACCOUNT OF	☐ OVER NIGHT TELEGRAM
	COLLECT			UNLESS BOX ABOVE IS CHECKED THIS MESSAGE WILL BE SENT AS A TELEGRAM

Send the following message, subject to the terms on back hereof, which are hereby agreed to

CARE OF OR APT. NO. **January 22** 19 73

TO **Sarah Weddington**
STREET & NO. **Weddington and Weddington**   TELEPHONE
709 West Fourteenth Street
CITY & STATE **Austin, Texas**   ZIP CODE **78701**

JUDGMENT ROE against WADE today AFFIRMED IN PART AND REVERSED IN

PART   JUDGMENT DOE against BOLTON MODIFIED AND AFFIRMED   Opinions

AIRMAILED

SENDER'S TEL. NO. **70-18 Appellants** NAME & ADDRESS   **Michael Rodak, Jr., Clerk**
ht
7D-4D   **Supreme Court of United States**

On January 22, 1973, the day the justices declared their rul-
ing on the Roe v. Wade *case, the above telegram was sent to*
Sarah Weddington at 709 West 14th Street in Austin, Texas.
Sent by clerk Michael Rodak Jr, the telegram states, "Judgment
Roe against Wade today affirmed in part and reversed in part
. . . Judgment Doe against Bolton modified and affirmed opin-
ions airmailed." From the collection of Sarah Weddington.

to decide that the right to choose an abortion was protected by
the Constitution," wrote Eva Rubin in *The Abortion Controversy*.
With the Supreme Court's ruling, the right to an abortion
became as protected as other rights given by the Constitution,
such as the right to free speech.

After Roe v. Wade

Usually a Supreme Court decision marks the end of a long legal struggle. In the case of *Roe v. Wade*, another fight was about to begin. The Supreme Court's ruling, "marked the beginning of a bitter battle between those who opposed abortion and those who supported a woman's right to choose," wrote Susan Dudley Gold in her book *Roe v. Wade*.

A NATION REACTS

Both sides of the abortion debate had strong reactions to the Court's decision. John Cardinal Krol of Philadelphia was the president of the National Conference of Catholic Bishops. He called the ruling "an unspeakable tragedy for this nation" in the *New York Times* the day after the decision.

Roe v. Wade

Antiabortion groups quickly began organizing an attempt to overturn the Court's ruling. They hoped to do several things to make abortion illegal once again. They planned to bring cases to court to challenge *Roe v. Wade*.

One main goal of these groups was to add a new amendment to the Constitution that gave legal rights to a fetus. Once a fetus has legal rights, *Roe v. Wade* could be constitutionally overturned. Antiabortion groups also hoped to get states to pass laws limiting abortions. The Supreme Court ruling had given states the right to make laws restricting abortion in the second and third trimesters. They hoped to make the laws as strict as possible. Antiabortion groups had an additional goal. They hoped to prevent the government from paying for abortions.

While many people were opposed to the *Roe v. Wade* decision, others were very happy about it. A *New York Times* editorial on January 23, 1973, called it a "major contribution to the preservation of individual liberties and of free decision-making." Groups like Planned Parenthood celebrated the decision. Now that abortion was legal, they decided to work to give women access to safe, inexpensive abortions.

Groups in favor of a woman's right to choose abortion knew they needed to work hard to keep abortion legal. They knew there would be many challenges to *Roe v. Wade*.

CHALLENGES TO THE NEW LAW

True to their goal of overturning *Roe*, antiabortion groups began bringing legal cases to try to change the laws. They

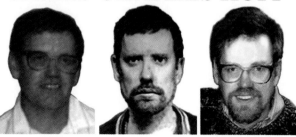

FBI TEN MOST WANTED FUGITIVE

VIOLATION OF THE FREEDOM OF ACCESS TO CLINIC ENTRANCES (FACE) ACT

JAMES CHARLES KOPP

Photograph taken in 1997 — Photograph taken in 1996

Aliases: James Kopp, Jim Kopp, John Doe, James Charles Copp, John Kapp, Clyde Swenson, Clyde Swanson, Jack Cotty, Jack Crotty, John Kopp, Jacob Koch, Charles Cooper, John Capp, Jim Cobb, James Cobb, Samuel E. Weinstein, Jacob I. Croninger, Enoch A. Guettler, Jonathan H. Henderson, Samuel E. Blanton, Soloman E. Aranburg, Aaron A. Bernstein, Eli A. Hochenleit, Dwight Hanson, K. Jawes Gavin, P. Anastation, B. James Milton, "Atomic Dog" and "Catfish"

This picture is from the 1999 FBI Ten Most Wanted List. It shows a photograph of the hunted murderer James Charles Kopp, who was wanted for the 1998 murder of Barnett Slepian, a doctor who performed abortions. Kopp was arrested in France in 2001 and convicted on March 18, 2003. Doctors who perform abortions can be targets for such antiabortion crusaders, who often will stop at nothing to make their case.

hoped to at least restrict abortion and possibly make it illegal once again.

The first case to challenge abortion laws did not go in favor of antiabortion groups. *Planned Parenthood v. Danforth* was decided in 1976. It stated that a woman's parents or husband could not prevent her from getting an abortion.

The next year, *Maher v. Roe* accomplished one of the goals of antiabortion groups. It said that women on welfare could not require the state to pay for an abortion.

Two abortion cases were decided in 1979. *Colautti v. Franklin* said that only doctors could decide when a fetus is

Even though abortion became legalized in the 1970s, this 1988 photo depicts an example of ongoing aggression from antiabortion protesters. Women entering the Atlanta Surgicenter, in Atlanta, Georgia, are protected by clinic escorts, who must walk inside police lines for their own safety. Protesters have a right to stage a demonstration, but they do not have the right to inflict harm on anyone or prevent clients from entering the clinic.

able to survive outside the mother. Courts would not be able to make that decision. *Belotti v. Baird* found that a state could make laws saying that women under age eighteen need permission from parents or a judge to get an abortion.

The 1989 case *Webster v. Reproductive Health Services* was a serious challenge to *Roe v. Wade*. The Supreme Court decision left women the right to abortion. However, it allowed states to create strict rules for women who wanted to get abortions. The ruling said states could prevent abortions from being performed in public hospitals or by doctors paid by public hospitals. States could also require a woman to have tests if she were more than

Michelle Featheringill, the CEO of Planned Parenthood New Mexico, walks with about forty other people in front of the Santa Fe, New Mexico, capitol building. Featheringill carries a sign that reads, "Keep Your Laws Off My Body." This march took place on January 22, 2002, the twenty-ninth anniversary of the United States Supreme Court's Roe v. Wade *decision.*

twenty weeks pregnant. If the tests showed that the fetus could live outside the mother, the abortion could be prevented.

The *Webster* decision worried pro-choice groups. They were concerned that the freedoms granted in *Roe v. Wade* might be taken away. These groups began organizing to ensure that the right to an abortion was not overturned.

Another challenge to *Roe* came in 1992. *Planned Parenthood v. Casey* upheld the right to an abortion. It also allowed states to continue placing restrictions on abortion.

Although the right to an abortion was still protected by the courts, antiabortion groups decided to try to make it difficult for women to obtain them. Protesters have marched in front of clinics where abortions are performed. In some cases, they have also resorted to violence. Several doctors who perform abortions have been shot, and even killed.

Some people are strongly opposed to abortion. Others support a woman's right to choose. People on both sides of the debate recognize that the *Roe v. Wade* decision was not only about abortion. As Weddington wrote in her autobiography, "[T]he Court's decision was an opportunity for all women. The battle was never 'for abortion'—abortion was not what we wanted to encourage. The battle was for the basic right of women to make their own decisions." For now, the freedom of choice remains protected by *Roe v. Wade*.

Glossary

abortion The termination of a pregnancy.

affidavit A legal document.

amendment A change or addition to a law.

appointed Chosen.

brief A statement of a lawyer's case that will be presented in court.

class action lawsuit A case filed on the behalf of many people.

concurring opinion A written statement agreeing with the decision but not the reasoning of the majority decision by a court of law.

constitutional Protected by the Constitution.

contraceptive A drug or device that prevents pregnancy.

controversial Causing strong disagreement.

dissenting opinion A written statement opposing the majority opinion by a court of law.

fetus A human baby developing in the womb of a mother.

justice   A judge.

opinion   The written statement of a decision by a court of law.

petition for certiorari   A document that asks the Supreme Court to take a case.

plaintiff   A person who files a lawsuit.

pollster   A person who conducts an official survey of opinions.

prosecute   To take legal action against someone accused of a crime.

resign   To give up a position.

trimester   A period of approximately three months into which a woman's pregnancy is divided.

For More Information

The Center for Reproductive Law and Policy (CRLP)

120 Wall Street

New York, NY 10005

(917) 637-3600

Web site: http://www.crlp.org

National Right to Life Committee

512 Tenth Street NW

Washington, DC 20004

(202) 626-8800

Web site: http://www.nrlc.org

Planned Parenthood Federation of America

810 Seventh Avenue

New York, NY 10019

(212) 541-7800

Web site: http://www.plannedparenthood.org

Web Sites

Due to the changing nature of Internet links, the Rosen Publishing Group, Inc., has developed an online list of Web sites related to the subject of this book. This site is updated regularly. Please use this link to access the list:

http://www.rosenlinks.com/scctps/rowa

For Further Reading

Andryszewski, Tricia. *Abortion: Rights, Options, Choices.* Brookfield, CT: The Millbrook Press, 1996.

The Center for Reproductive Law and Policy. *Roe v. Wade and the Right to Privacy.* New York: The Center for Reproductive Law and Policy, 2001.

Gold, Susan Dudley. *Roe v. Wade.* New York: Twenty-First Century Books, 1994.

Herda, D. J. *Roe v. Wade: The Abortion Question.* Berkeley Heights, NJ: Enslow Publishers Inc., 1994.

Romaine, Deborah S. *Roe v. Wade: Abortion and the Supreme Court.* San Diego: Lucent Books, 1998.

Stevens, Leonard A. *The Case of Roe v. Wade.* New York: G. P. Putnam's Sons, 1996.

Tompkins, Nancy. *Roe v. Wade: The Fight Over Life and Liberty.* New York: Franklin Watts, 1996.

Bibliography

The Center for Reproductive Law and Policy. *Roe v. Wade and the Right to Privacy*. New York: The Center for Reproductive Law and Policy, 2001.

CNN Interactive. "Special Report: *Roe v. Wade* Twenty-five Years Later," 1998. Retrieved October 10, 2002 (http://www.cnn.com/SPECIALS/1998/roe.wade).

Faux, Marian. *Roe v. Wade: The Untold Story of the Landmark Supreme Court Decision that Made Abortion Legal*. Rev. ed. New York: Cooper Square Press, 2001.

Gold, Susan Dudley. *Roe v. Wade*. New York: Twenty-First Century Books, 1994.

Hull, N. E. H., and Peter Charles Hoffer, eds. *Roe v. Wade: The Abortion Rights Controversy in American History*. Lawrence, KS: The University Press of Kansas, 2001.

McCorvey, Norma, with Andy Meisler. *I Am Roe: My Life, Roe v. Wade, and Freedom of Choice*. New York: HarperCollins Publishers, 1994.

PBS Online Forum. "*Roe v. Wade*: What Is the Legal Legacy of the 1973 Supreme Court Decision on Abortion?" January 30, 1998. Retrieved October 10, 2002 (http://www.pbs.org/newshour/forum/january98/roe_1-30.html).

Rubin, Eva S., ed. *The Abortion Controversy: A Documentary History.* Westport, CT: Praeger, 1998.

Stevens, Leonard A. *The Case of Roe v. Wade.* New York: G. P. Putnam's Sons, 1996.

Tompkins, Nancy. *Roe v. Wade: The Fight Over Life and Liberty.* New York: Franklin Watts, 1996.

Weddington, Sarah. *A Question of Choice.* New York: G. P. Putnam's Sons, 1992.

Primary Source Image List

Cover: Photograph of abortion activists outside the U.S. Supreme Court. Taken by an Associated Press photographer in Washington, DC, on June 30, 1992.

Page 5: Photograph of pro-choice picketers in Fort Mitchell, Kentucky. Taken by Mark Meyer in 1979. Photograph of man wearing anti-abortion sign. Taken in 1976 in Boston, Massachusetts, by Owen Franken.

Page 8: Photograph of Margaret Sanger. Taken in Washington, D.C., on March 1, 1934, by an Associated Press photographer.

Page 9: Photograph of police taking woman out of Dr. Louis Solomon's apartment. Taken in 1944.

Page 10: Penal code of the state of Texas. Created in 1857. Found at the Texas State Library in Austin, Texas.

Page 11: Photograph of Sarah Weddington. Taken in Texas by an Associated Press photographer.

Page 13: Photograph of Linda Coffee. Taken on February 7, 1972, in Dallas, Texas.

Page 17: Photograph of Norma McCorvey. Taken in Terrel, Texas, by an Associated Press photographer on January 21, 1983.

Page 18: Photograph of pro-choice demonstration. Taken in New York City in 1972.

Page 21: Photograph of Henry Wade. Taken in Dallas, Texas, in the early 1970s by an Associated Press photographer.

Page 30: Photograph of the interior of the Supreme Court in Washington, D.C. Housed in the Collection of the Supreme Court of the United States.

Page 31: Photograph of Ron Weddington, Sarah Weddington, George Mahon, and Lena Katharine Ragle. Taken in Washington, D.C., on December 13, 1971. From the collection of Sarah Weddington.

Page 34: Photograph of abortion billboard. Taken in McGrann, Pennsylvania, on April 13, 1971.

Page 35: Photograph of Warren Burger. Taken in 1971 in Washington, D.C., by Robert Oakes. From the Collection of the Supreme Court of the United States.

Page 38: Photograph of Supreme Court justices. Taken by Robert Oakes in Washington, D.C. From the collection of the Supreme Court of the United States.

Page 40: Cartoon of graveyard. Drawn by Steve Breen. Printed in the Asbury Park Press.

Page 41: Cartoon of the Constitution in a gun sight. Drawn by Kevin Siers. Printed in the Charlotte Observer in 1998.

Page 43: Photograph of Harry Blackmun. Taken on February 4, 1974, in St. Paul, Minnesota.

Page 45: Signed Supreme Court syllabus for the Roe v. Wade decision. January 22, 1973. From the collection of Sarah Weddington.

Page 46: Telegram to Sarah Weddington from the U.S. Supreme Court. Created January 22, 1973. From the collection of Sarah Weddington.

Page 49: Poster of James Charles Kopp on FBI Ten Most Wanted. Created in 1999 in New York City.

Page 50: Photograph of abortion clinic escorts. Taken in Atlanta, Georgia, on October 4, 1988.

Page 51: Photograph of Michelle Featheringill with pro-choice demonstrators. Taken in Santa Fe, New Mexico, on January 22, 2002, by Sarah Martone.

Index

A

abortion

    challenges to laws against, 5–6, 11–12, 21

    controversy and, 4, 6, 36, 44

    history of, 4, 7–9

    laws about, 4, 8, 9, 10, 11, 16–17, 19, 21, 29, 33–34, 38, 42, 48, 49–51

    and safety, 8–9, 10–11, 12, 17, 22, 38, 48

Abortion Controversy, The (Rubin), 46

abortions, illegal, 4, 8, 14

American Civil Liberties Union (ACLU), 28

amicus curiae briefs, 28, 29

antiabortion opinions/arguments, 4, 8, 42, 47, 51–52

appeals, 25

Austin, Texas, 10, 11

B

Beasley, Dorothy, 32

Belotti v. Baird, 50

birth defects, 9

Blackmun, Harry, 30, 36, 42–43, 44

Brandeis, Louis, 17, 18

Brennan, William, 30

briefs, 19, 26–28, 29, 37

Brown, John R., 22

Burger, Warren, 30, 35, 36, 37

C

Catholics, 42, 47

class action lawsuit, 19, 33

Coffee, Linda

    agrees to take *Roe* case, 13

    appeal to Supreme Court, 25, 26

    and federal court case, 19, 21, 22

preparing for federal trial,
14–15, 16, 18
preparing for Supreme Court
case, 26–28, 29
Colautti v. Franklin, 49–50
Congress, 30
Connecticut, 8, 18

D
Dallas, Texas, 13, 14, 19, 21
Doe v. Bolton, 32
Douglas, William, 30
due process, 20

F
fetus, rights of, 6, 21–22, 23, 28,
32, 33, 34, 38–40, 44, 48
Fifth Amendment, 19, 20
First Amendment, 19, 20
Flowers, Robert, 39–40
Floyd, Jay, 28, 32–35, 37
founding fathers, 17
Fourteenth Amendment, 19, 20,
32, 44
Fourth Amendment, 19, 20
Frazel, Jerome, 28

G
Gold, Susan Dudley, 47
Griswold v. Connecticut, 18–19

H
Hames, Margie Pitts, 32
Horan, Dennis, 28

J
James Madison Constitutional
Law Institute, 27

K
Knights of Columbus, 42
Krol, John Cardinal, 47

L
"Ladies' Day," 32
Lucas, Roy, 27

M
Maher v. Roe, 49
Marshall, Thurgood, 30
McCorvey, Norma (Jane Roe),
5–6, 14–15, 16, 19, 20, 21,
23, 24, 33
Mexico, 10, 12
moot courts, 28
mother, rights of, 6, 17, 21–22, 23,
28, 34, 38–39, 41, 44, 52

N
National Conference of Catholic
Bishops, 47
New Jersey, 42

New York, 27, 38, 39, 42

Ninth Amendment, 17–18, 19,
    20, 23, 32

O

opinions, Supreme Court, 36, 43
    concurring, 36, 43, 44
    dissenting, 36, 43, 45

P

petition for certiorari, 26

Planned Parenthood, 9, 28,
    48, 49

Planned Parenthood v. Casey, 51

Planned Parenthood v. Danforth, 49

Powell, Lewis, 37

privacy, right to, 6, 17, 18, 19, 20,
    22, 23, 38, 44, 45

pro-choice opinions/
    arguments, 4, 9, 31–32,
    48, 51, 52

Q

Question of Choice, A
    (Weddington), 7, 12, 52

R

rape, 9

Rehnquist, William, 37, 45

Roe, Jane (Norma McCorvey), 5–6,
    14–15, 16, 19, 20, 21, 23,
    24, 33

Roe v. Wade
    challenges to, 48–51
    in federal court, 22–24
    history of, 4–6
    reaction to, 47–48
    in Supreme Court, 25, 26–36,
        37–41

Roe v. Wade (book by Gold), 47

Rubin, Eva, 46

S

Stewart, Potter, 30, 44

Supreme Court, 4, 6, 17, 18, 50
    justices of, 30
    and *Roe v. Wade* decision,
        35–36, 43–46, 47
    and *Roe v. Wade* first hearing,
        25–26, 28, 29–36
    and *Roe v. Wade* second
        hearing, 37–41

T

Texas
    abortion laws in, 5–6, 10–11,
        16–17, 19, 21, 22, 23–24, 25,
        33–34
    and *Roe v. Wade*, 28, 29, 33–34,
        39, 40

Third Amendment, 19

Tolle, John, 21–22, 23

trimesters of pregnancy, 43, 44, 48

U

University of Texas Law School, 11, 13

U.S. Constitution
amendments to, 19, 20, 26, 48
and rights of fetus, 32, 38, 39, 48
and right to choose, 40, 43, 45–46
and right to privacy, 16–18, 44, 45
and Supreme Court decisions, 25–26

V

Vermont, 42

W

Wade, Henry, 19–21, 24, 28
Webster v. Reproductive Health Services, 50–51

Weddington, Ron, 12, 27
Weddington, Sarah
agrees to take *Roe* case, 11–12
appeal to Supreme Court, 25, 26
autobiography of, 7, 12, 52
and federal court case, 19, 21, 22
preparing for federal trial, 13, 14–15, 16, 18
preparing for Supreme Court case, 26–28
speaking before Supreme Court, 29, 31–32, 37–39, 40–41, 44
White, Byron, 30, 43, 45
Women's Liberation Birth Control Information Center, 10–11
women's movement, 21

About the Author

Simone Payment has a degree in psychology from Cornell University and a master's degree in elementary education from Wheelock College. She is also the author of a biography of the Negro League baseball star Buck Leonard, a biography of the French explorer La Salle, and books about travel careers and Navy SEALs.

Acknowledgments

The author would like to thank Howard Cooper and Lori Cooper for their valuable insights, suggestions, and continued support.

Photo Credits

Royalty Free images throughout: Eagle on back cover and through-out interior © Eyewire; Red curtain throughout interior © Arthur S. Aubry/PhotoDisc; Wood grain on cover and back cover and throughout interior © M. Angelo/Corbis; Cover, pp. 8, 11, 17, 21, 51 © AP/Wide World Photos; p. 5 (left) © Mark Meyer/TimePix; p. 5 (right) © Owen Franken/Corbis; p. 9, 13, 34, 43, 50 © Bettmann/Corbis; p. 10 Legislative Reference Library of Texas, Austin, TX; p. 18 © Charles Gatewood/The Image Works, Inc.; p. 30 Franz Jantzen/Collection of the Supreme Court of the United States; pp. 31, 45, 46 from the collection of Sarah Weddington; pp. 35, 38 Robert Oakes/Collection of the Supreme Court of the United States; p. 40 © Steve Breen/Asbury Park Press; p. 41 reprinted with special permission of North American Syndicate; p. 49 © Reuters/TimePix.

Designer: Evelyn Horovicz; Editor: Christine Poolos;
Photo Researcher: Amy Feinberg